SOCCER WORLD CUP

Clive Gifford

 Crabtree Publishing Company

www.crabtreebooks.com

Crabtree Publishing Company

www.crabtreebooks.com   1-800-387-7650
Copyright © **2009 CRABTREE PUBLISHING COMPANY**.

**Published
in Canada
Crabtree Publishing**
616 Welland Ave.
St. Catharines, ON
L2M 5V6

**Published in the
United States
Crabtree Publishing**
PMB16A
350 Fifth Ave., Suite 3308
New York, NY 10118

Content development by Shakespeare Squared
www.ShakespeareSquared.com

Author: Clive Gifford
Project editor: Ruth Owen
Project designer: Simon Fenn
Photo research: Ruth Owen
Project coordinator: Robert Walker
Production coordinator: Katherine Berti
Prepress technicians: Katherine Berti,
    Ken Wright

Thank you to
Lorraine Petersen
and the members
of nasen

Picture credits:
Empics Wire Pic: p. 21 (bottom)
Getty Images: p. 11 (left), 13, 16–17, 18, 24, 26, 27; AFP: p. 2–3,
    5 (top and bottom), 8–9, 11 (right), 14, 19, 23, 28–29, 31;
    Bongarts: p. 4, 6–7, 22; Stu Forster/Allsport: p. 15
Rex Features: Sipa Press: front cover
Shutterstock: p. 1, 10, 12, 20, 21 (top), 29 (top)

Every effort has been made to trace copyright holders, and we apologize in
advance for any omissions. We would be pleased to insert the appropriate
acknowledgments in any subsequent edition of this publication.

Library and Archives Canada Cataloguing in Publication

Gifford, Clive
    Soccer World Cup / Clive Gifford.

(Crabtree contact)
Includes index.
ISBN 978-0-7787-3778-0 (bound).--ISBN 978-0-7787-3800-8 (pbk.)

        1. World Cup (Soccer)--Juvenile literature. I. Title.
II. Series: Crabtree contact

GV943.49.G53 2009   j796.334'668   C2008-907860-8

Library of Congress Cataloging-in-Publication Data

Gifford, Clive.
    Soccer World Cup / Clive Gifford.
        p. cm. -- (Crabtree contact)
    Includes index.
    ISBN 978-0-7787-3800-8 (pbk. : alk. paper) -- ISBN 978-0-
7787-3778-0 (reinforced library binding : alk. paper)
    1. World Cup (Soccer) I. Title. II. Series.

    GV943.49.G45 2009
    796.334'668--dc22

                                                    2008052389

CONTENTS

THE BIG ONE

The **FIFA** World Cup is the biggest soccer competition on Earth.

Every four years, 32 national teams take part in the World Cup finals.

The action, drama, and goals are watched by over one billion people on TV.

The 2006 World Cup Final between Italy and France.

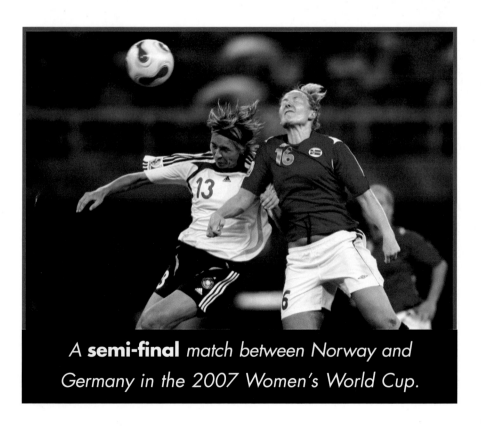

A **semi-final** match between Norway and Germany in the 2007 Women's World Cup.

Only seven teams have ever won the World Cup.

THE ULTIMATE PRIZE

This is it! The ultimate prize—the FIFA World Cup Trophy. The trophy is made of gold.

FIFA WORLD CUP TROPHY FACTS

- The trophy was made in 1970
- Weight—13.6 pounds (6.17 kg)
- Height—14.5 inches (36.8 cm)
- All the winners since 1974 are engraved on the base

The first World Cup trophy was called the "Jules Rimet Cup." It had an eventful life.

During World War II, the cup was hidden in a shoebox under the bed of an Italian soccer official. This was to prevent it from being stolen by German soldiers.

In 1966, the cup was stolen just before the tournament. A small dog named Pickles found it buried under a tree!

When Brazil won the cup for the third time, they were able to keep it. In 1983, it was stolen. The thieves melted it down for the gold.

Today, the winning team only gets a copy of the FIFA World Cup Trophy. They do not get the real gold one!

HOSTS

FIFA chooses which country will **host** a World Cup tournament. Being the host is a big deal.

New **stadiums** have to be built.

Several million soccer fans need a way to get to and from the games. They also need food and places to stay. Extra police are needed to keep things running smoothly.

FUTURE HOSTS

In 2010, South Africa will host the World Cup finals.
In 2014, it will be Brazil.

*This is the International Stadium Yokohama in Japan.
In 2002, 69,000 fans packed the stadium for the
World Cup Final match between Germany and Brazil.*

Fans flock to the World Cup finals. They want to watch their soccer heroes in action.

The most fans that ever crammed into one stadium was 199,854. The event was the 1950 World Cup Final match between Brazil and Uruguay. The match was played in the Maracana Stadium in Brazil.

ATTENDANCE NUMBERS

Year	Host Country	FIFA Total Attendance
2006	Germany	3,359,439
2002	Korea/Japan	2,705,197
1998	France	2,785,100
1994	USA	3,587,538
1990	Italy	2,516,348

At the 2002 World Cup finals, Japanese player Tsuneyasu Miyamoto wore a mask. He wore it to protect his face.

Thousands of Japanese fans copied their favorite player.

GETTING TO THE FINALS

Over 200 countries try to get their teams into the World Cup finals.

Teams play matches called **qualifiers**.
If a team wins enough matches, it will qualify to be one of the 32 teams to play in the finals.

*2005—Fans in Angola, Africa, celebrate their team qualifying for the 2006 World Cup finals.
It was the first time Angola had qualified.*

Miss out on qualifying,
and it's heartbreak!

THRASHED!

Archie Thompson

Match:
2001 World Cup qualifier
Teams:
Australia vs American Samoa
Score:
31–0 to Australia
Top Scorer:
Archie Thompson with 13 goals

THE TOURNAMENT

Six tough games stand between a team and a World Cup Final.

Months before the tournament starts, the **group draw** is made at a special event.

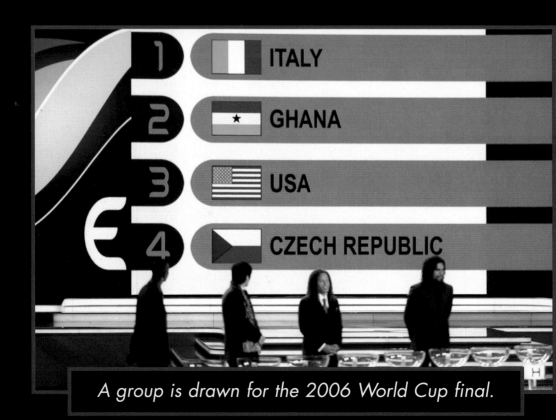

A group is drawn for the 2006 World Cup final.

Games are now knockout. The pressure is really on.

The 16 teams play in eight matches. The eight winning teams go through to the quarter finals. The losing teams go home.

1998—France celebrate winning their **quarter finals** game against Italy.

The winners of the quarter finals go through to the semi-finals.

Finally, there are just two teams left.

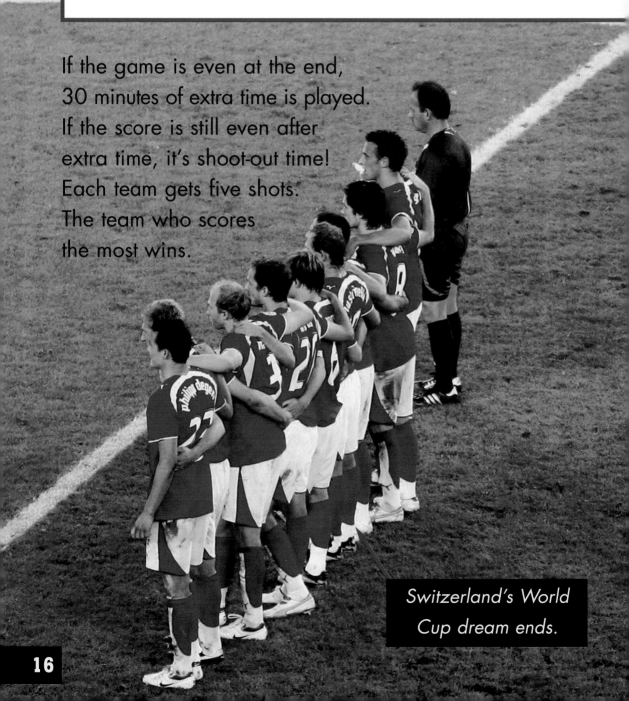

SHOOT-OUTS

In the elimination rounds of the tournament, a game cannot end with a draw. One team must lose—and leave the tournament.

If the game is even at the end,
30 minutes of extra time is played.
If the score is still even after
extra time, it's shoot-out time!
Each team gets five shots.
The team who scores
the most wins.

*Switzerland's World
Cup dream ends.*

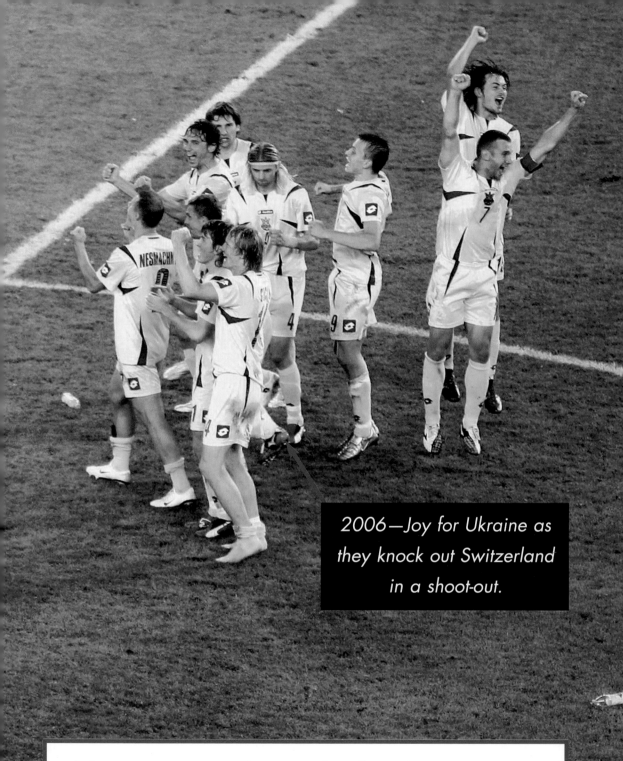

2006—Joy for Ukraine as they knock out Switzerland in a shoot-out.

If the scores are still even after five shots each, the teams continue on until one team misses!

There have been 20 shoot-outs in World Cup finals.

WINNERS

There have been 18 World Cup tournaments. Only seven teams have won the World Cup.

Six World Cups have been won by the team hosting the tournament.

WORLD CUP WINNERS

- Brazil—5 times
- Italy—4 times
- Germany—3 times
- Argentina—twice
- Uruguay—twice
- England—once
- France—once

1966—England beat Germany in the World Cup Final held in London, England.

" To hold the World Cup in my hands is one of the most incredible moments in my life. **"**

Brazilian striker Ronaldo

2002—Brazil's Ronaldo battles it out against Germany in the World Cup final.

ALL-TIME GREAT

Only one player has won as a team captain (1974) and later, as a coach (1990). That man is Franz Beckenbauer of Germany.

BRILLIANT BRAZIL

Brazil is the best. No question!
They have won the World Cup five times
and reached the semi-finals 10 times.

Brazil is the only team to have qualified
and played in every single World Cup.

	Played	Won	Drawn	Lost	Goals Scored
1. Brazil	92	64	14	14	201
2. Germany	92	55	19	18	190
3. Italy	77	44	19	14	122

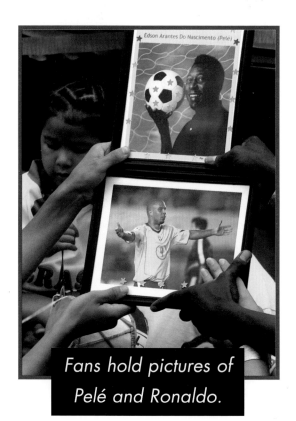

Fans hold pictures of Pelé and Ronaldo.

Brazilian player Pelé is the only three-time World Cup winner. He was on the winning team in 1958, 1962, and 1970.

Brazil's Ronaldo is the top World Cup scorer. He has scored a total of 15 goals in World Cup tournaments.

1970—Pelé celebrates scoring the first goal in the World Cup Final between Brazil and Italy.

WOMEN'S WORLD CUP

The FIFA Women's World Cup began in 1991. Teams from 16 countries take part.

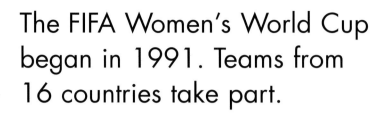

Germany's 2007 win earned the team one million dollars in prize money.

The team didn't let a single goal in during the tournament. In their opening game, Germany beat Argentina 11–0. That's a World Cup record.

2007—Birgit Prinz of Germany scores her third goal against Argentina.

Two players have appeared at all five Women's World Cups:

- Bente Nordby—Goalkeeper (Norway)
- Kristine Lilly—**Midfielder** (U.S.)

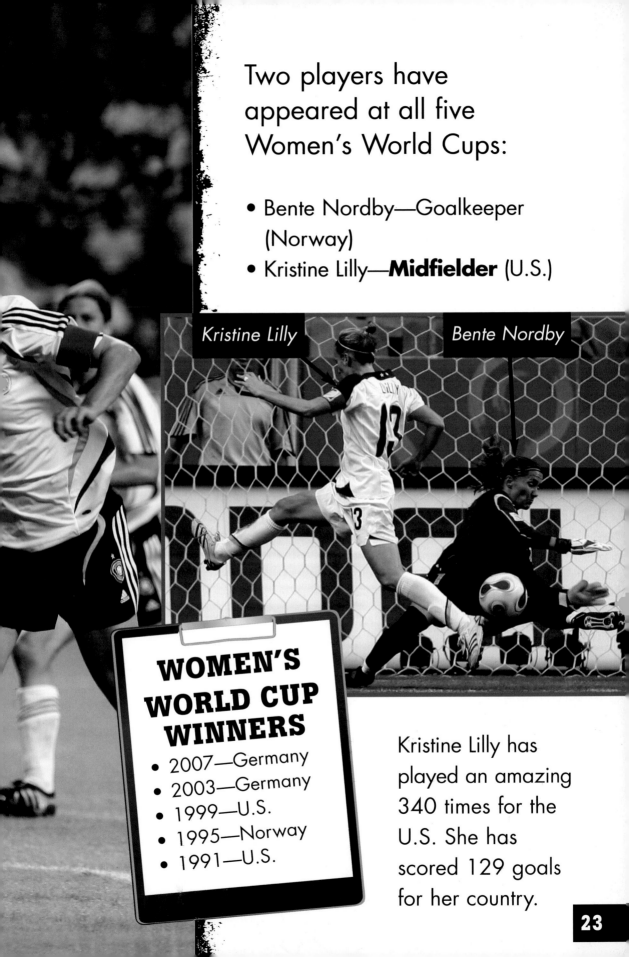

Kristine Lilly

Bente Nordby

WOMEN'S WORLD CUP WINNERS

- 2007—Germany
- 2003—Germany
- 1999—U.S.
- 1995—Norway
- 1991—U.S.

Kristine Lilly has played an amazing 340 times for the U.S. She has scored 129 goals for her country.

WORLD CUP WONDERS

MOST APPEARANCES

Lothar Matthäus, Germany   25
Paolo Maldini, Italy   23
Diego Maradona, Argentina   21

FASTEST GOALS

Hakan Sükür of Turkey
   11 seconds—2002
Vaclav Masek of Czechoslovakia
   15 seconds—1962

TOP GOALSCORERS

Ronaldo, Brazil   15
Gerd Müller, Germany   14
Juste Fontaine, France   13
Pelé, Brazil   12
Sandor Kocsis, Hungary   11
Jürgen Klinsmann, Germany   11

The most **red cards** in one match was four. The game was between Portugal and the Netherlands in 2006.

REFEREES

Being a referee is hard. Being a World Cup referee is really difficult.

The whole world is watching.

You don't want to make a mistake...

...like English referee Graham Poll did in 2006.

He gave a **yellow card** to Josip Simunic of Croatia three times. You should be sent off the field if you get two yellows.

346 The most yellow cards at one World Cup in 2006.

Jean Langenus was the referee at the first World Cup Final in 1930.

He didn't wear black like today's referees. He wore horseriding trousers, a dinner jacket, and tie!

142 The total number of red cards in all World Cups.

56 The number of seconds José Batista of Uruguay was on the field before he was sent off in 1986.

SURPRISE!

Shocks happen! That's what's so great about the World Cup.

At the 2002 World Cup, South Korea knocked out favorite Italy in the early stages. Ahn Jung Hwan scored for South Korea. However, Hwan played for an Italian soccer club. He was not very popular back in Italy!

2002—South Korea celebrate their surprise win!

At the 1950 World Cup, England was a top team. But the US beat them 1–0.

WINNING STREAK

Bulgaria had never won a game in a World Cup tournament.

In 1994, Bulgaria beat Greece, Argentina, Mexico, and Germany in a row to reach the semi-finals.

Switzerland	GREATEST COMEBACK—1954	Austria
3	At half time	**0**
Switzerland		Austria
5	Final score	**7**

NEED-TO-KNOW WORDS

FIFA The organization that runs world soccer competitions. FIFA was formed in 1904

group draw When the 32 teams that reach the World Cup finals are put into eight groups of four. The teams are drawn at random at a special event

host The act of holding and running the World Cup final. Also the word for the country which holds the World Cup final

mascot A cartoon-like character or object that represents a soccer club or a World Cup tournament

midfielder A player who plays in the middle of the field and is skilled in attack and defense

qualifier One of a series of matches played by teams with the aim of getting to the World Cup finals

quarter finals Four matches played by the last eight teams in a tournament

red card A card shown by a referee to send a player off the field

semi-finals Two matches played by the last four teams in a tournament. The two winning teams play each other in the final

stadium The building which holds a soccer field and seats for thousands of spectators

yellow card A card shown by a referee to a player as a warning

MASCOT MANIA

The first World Cup **mascot** appeared in 1966. He was a dog called World Cup Willie. There have been some strange mascots since then.

- A giant orange in Spain in 1982
- A chili pepper wearing a moustache and sombrero hat in Mexico in 1986
- A lion and talking soccer ball in Germany in 2006

The 2006 mascot Goleo and the talking ball Pille.

WORLD CUP ONLINE

www.fifa.com/worldcup/index.html

www.planetworldcup.com/

www.fifaworldcup.co.uk/

news.bbc.co.uk/sport1/hi/football/world_cup_2006/default.stm

Publisher's note to educators and parents:
Our editors have carefully reviewed these websites to ensure that they are suitable for children. Many websites change frequently, however, and we cannot guarantee that a site's future contents will continue to meet our high standards of quality and educational value. Be advised that children should be closely supervised whenever they access the Internet.

INDEX